Urban Exploration - Amsterdam The Comprehensive Travel Guide

PA BOOKS

Published by PA BOOKS, 2023.

URBAN EXPLORATION - AMSTERDAM THE COMPREHENSIVE TRAVEL GUIDE

First edition. October 29, 2023.

Copyright © 2023 PA BOOKS.

ISBN: 979-8223085515

Written by PA BOOKS.

Also by PA BOOKS

Hogan's Key

Kimberly & the Five Strange Goldfishes

The Enchanted Library

The Misadventures of Pirate Pete

From Wheel To Web: 40 Remarkable Inventions

Once Upon A Sleepy Time

The Global Game - The Evolution Of Football

Strides To Success: A Beginner's Guide to Running

The ChatGPT Handbook

Climate Crossroads

1000 Everyday Life Hacks

Urban Exploration - London The Comprehensive Travel Guide

Urban Exploration - New York The Comprehensive Travel Guide

Urban Exploration - Amsterdam The Comprehensive Travel Guide

Urban Exploration - Dubai The Comprehensive Travel Guide

Urban Exploration - Paris The Comprehensive Travel Guide

Table of Contents

Chapter 1: Introduction to Amsterdam 1

Chapter 2: Navigating Amsterdam 5

Chapter 3: Hidden Gems in the City Center 11

Chapter 4: Amsterdam's Canal District 15

Chapter 5: Local Culture and Traditions 19

Chapter 6: The Unique Neighbourhoods 25

Chapter 7: Amsterdam's Hidden Waterways 31

Chapter 8: Amsterdam's Artistic Heritage 35

Chapter 9: Amsterdam's Cultural Festivals 43

Chapter 10: Amsterdam's Culinary Odyssey 47

Chapter 11: Amsterdam by Night 51

Chapter 12: Amsterdam's Green Escapes 57

Chapter 1: Introduction to Amsterdam

Welcome to the enchanting city of Amsterdam! Nestled in the heart of the Netherlands, this vibrant metropolis is a treasure trove of history, culture, and hidden gems waiting to be discovered. As you embark on your urban exploration journey, let's delve into the essence of Amsterdam, providing you with essential insights to make the most of your visit.

A Brief Overview

Amsterdam, often referred to as the "Venice of the North" due to its extensive canal system, is a city like no other. With its rich history, charming architecture, and a unique cultural blend, this city has captivated the hearts of travellers from around the world for centuries. As you wander its picturesque streets and waterways, you'll soon understand why.

A City of Diversity

Amsterdam is a melting pot of diversity, where the old and the new, the traditional and the modern coexist harmoniously. It is a city that embraces people from all walks of life, creating an atmosphere that is both welcoming and inclusive. Whether you're an art enthusiast, a foodie, a history buff, or a nature lover, Amsterdam has something to offer everyone.

A Tourist Haven

Amsterdam is not only a hub for urban explorers but also a top destination for tourists worldwide. Its enduring popularity can be attributed to its vibrant culture, historic significance, and an array of attractions. As you navigate its bustling streets, keep in mind that there's more to this city than what meets the eye. It's not just about visiting the well-known landmarks, but also about uncovering the city's hidden gems, local traditions, and the lesser-explored neighbourhoods.

Urban Exploration: A Unique Perspective

In this guide, we're going to approach Amsterdam with a different lens. Rather than just scratching the surface, we'll delve deep into the city's neighbourhoods, culture, and history. Urban exploration offers a unique way to experience the soul of Amsterdam, allowing you to connect with the city and its people on a more intimate level. As you roam through the winding streets and canal banks, you'll encounter a side of Amsterdam that many tourists miss. This guide will help you become an Amsterdam insider.

What to Expect

In the chapters that follow, we will guide you through Amsterdam's hidden gems, local culture, and unique neighbourhoods, providing detailed insights, recommendations, and local tips to enhance your exploration. From the bustling city centre to the tranquil outskirts, we'll cover it all. Expect to discover the best spots for street art, hidden courtyards, historic buildings, and so much more.

Navigation

Navigating the city is essential for an enjoyable experience. We will provide tips on transportation options, including trams, buses, and cycling, which is a beloved mode of travel in Amsterdam. We'll also discuss the layout of the canals and neighbourhoods to help you get your bearings, ensuring you make the most of your time exploring.

The Adventure Begins

With a rich tapestry of history, diverse culture, and captivating neighbourhoods, Amsterdam is the ideal city for urban exploration. Join us on this adventure, as we unveil the city's best-kept secrets and provide you with the tools to create a memorable experience. Get ready to explore Amsterdam's hidden treasures, absorb its local culture, and immerse yourself in its unique neighbourhoods. Your journey of urban exploration begins now.

Chapter 2: Navigating Amsterdam

In order to fully immerse yourself in the urban exploration of Amsterdam, it's crucial to understand how to navigate this magnificent city. From its intricate network of canals to the various modes of transportation at your disposal, this chapter will serve as your compass, helping you make the most of your journey.

The Canal-Crossed Maze

Amsterdam's distinct charm arises from its 165 captivating canals, which crisscross the city in a web of watery pathways. It's essential to grasp the layout of this unique urban landscape.

Canal Rings: The heart of Amsterdam consists of three canal rings - the Herengracht (Gentlemen's Canal), Keizersgracht (Emperor's Canal), and Prinsengracht (Prince's Canal). These concentric canals are a UNESCO World Heritage site and form the city's historic centre. Around these canals, you'll discover a wealth of hidden treasures, from courtyards to architectural gems.

De Pijp: This lively neighbourhood in the south of Amsterdam offers a different canal experience. The Albert Cuyp Market and the Sarphatipark are among the hidden gems waiting to be explored here.

Jordaan: A short walk from the central station takes you to the Jordaan district. Its picturesque canals and quaint bridges provide an idyllic backdrop for urban exploration.

Oud-West: Venture to the west of the city centre, and you'll find the Oud-West neighbourhood, known for its charming canals like Kostverlorenvaart and Admiralengracht.

Transportation Options

Amsterdam offers a variety of transportation options to help you navigate its streets, canals, and neighbourhoods with ease.

Bicycles: One of the most iconic ways to get around Amsterdam is by bike. The city is incredibly bike-friendly, with dedicated bike lanes and bike-sharing programs. Blend in with the locals, rent a bicycle, and embark on your exploration. You'll find bike rental shops throughout the city, making it convenient to hop on two wheels.

Trams and Buses: Amsterdam's public transportation system is efficient and extensive, serving the city and its suburbs. Trams and buses are perfect for traveling longer distances within Amsterdam and exploring areas not easily reached by bike.

Walking: Amsterdam is a pedestrian-friendly city with plenty of sidewalks and crosswalks. Walking allows you to absorb the city's unique atmosphere and stumble upon hidden gems that you might otherwise miss.

Canal Cruises: To gain a different perspective of the city, consider taking a canal cruise. These leisurely boat rides provide an excellent way to explore Amsterdam from its waterways. Various canal cruise operators offer a range of tours, including day and night options.

Navigating the Canals

As you wander along the canal banks, you'll notice that each street is lined with a series of characteristic houses. Pay attention to the house numbers; they are essential for locating addresses in Amsterdam. Odd numbers are typically found on the left side of the canal, while even numbers are on the right.

Each canal is adorned with picturesque bridges, many of which have their unique history and design. Take your time to cross these bridges and capture the perfect photo while savouring the stunning views of the canals.

Getting Around with Trams and Buses

Amsterdam's trams and buses are an efficient way to explore the city's various neighbourhoods. Trams are easily recognizable, with their distinctive white and blue colours. Tram lines crisscross the city, providing excellent connectivity to many attractions and neighbourhoods.

Bus services are comprehensive, and you can use them to access places that may be further from the city centre. Public transportation operates on a chip card system, and you can purchase travel cards for convenience. Make sure to check the timetables and routes to plan your journey effectively.

Biking the City

Amsterdam is renowned for its cycling culture, and biking is undoubtedly one of the most enjoyable and efficient ways to get around. The city's flat terrain, dedicated bike lanes, and traffic regulations that favour cyclists make it an ideal destination for pedalling. You can rent a bike from numerous rental shops in the city, or you might even consider using bike-sharing programs.

Navigational Apps and Maps

To enhance your navigation, consider using navigation apps such as Google Maps, which provides real-time information on public transportation schedules and cycling routes. Alternatively, you can pick up physical maps at information centres and hotels.

Safety and Etiquette

When exploring Amsterdam, it's important to follow safety and etiquette guidelines. While cycling, always adhere to traffic rules, and be mindful of pedestrians. Lock your bike securely when not in use, as bike theft can be a concern.

When using public transportation, be respectful of other passengers and ensure you have a valid ticket. Additionally, keep an eye on your belongings, as crowded trams and buses can present opportunities for pickpockets.

Summary

Navigating Amsterdam is an integral part of your urban exploration adventure. The city's canals, bicycles, trams, and buses all play a crucial role in making your journey memorable. Understanding the layout, transportation options, and navigation tips will help you explore Amsterdam with ease and discover its hidden treasures. So, with your compass in hand, it's time to embark on your Amsterdam adventure. The next chapters will delve into specific aspects of the city to enhance your exploration further.

Chapter 3: Hidden Gems in the City Center

Welcome to the heart of Amsterdam, where centuries of history, enchanting architecture, and hidden gems await your urban exploration. In this chapter, we'll guide you through the lesser-known treasures of the city centre, revealing pockets of culture, history, and intrigue that are often overshadowed by the more famous attractions. Be well-equipped to unearth the secrets of Amsterdam's core.

Discovering Hidden Courtyards

Amsterdam's city centre is a treasure chest of hidden courtyards, often concealed behind Grand Canal houses and unassuming doorways. These hidden oases offer a glimpse into the city's historical charm and provide a tranquil escape from the bustling streets.

1. Begijnhof: Tucked away behind a heavy wooden door, the Begijnhof is a serene courtyard with quaint houses surrounding a lush garden. This hidden gem is an oasis of calm in the heart of the city, and its home to the English Reformed Church, one of the oldest wooden houses in Amsterdam, and a chapel dating back to the 15th century.

2. Museum Van Loon Garden: Located on Keizersgracht, the Museum Van Loon is a canal house museum with a beautiful garden in the back. This peaceful green space, complete with a charming tea house, provides a peaceful retreat in the city centre.

Historical House Museums

Amsterdam's house museums offer a unique opportunity to step back in time and explore the life of Amsterdam's wealthy and influential residents. These often-overlooked gems provide an intimate look into the city's past.

1. Museum Geelvinck-Hinlopen Huis: Situated on the picturesque Herengracht, this hidden gem offers a glimpse into the grandeur of a 17th-century canal house. It showcases a remarkable collection of period furniture, silverware, and musical instruments.

2. Museum Willet-Holthuysen: Housed in an opulent canal house on Herengracht, this museum offers a rare peek into the life of a prosperous Amsterdam couple during the 18th century. The rooms are meticulously decorated, and the garden is a tranquil haven.

Quirky and Unique Museums

Amsterdam is renowned for its museums, and while world-famous institutions like the Rijksmuseum and Van Gogh Museum are must-visit destinations, the city centre boasts a range of smaller, quirky museums that are well worth your time.

1. Electric Ladyland – The Museum of Fluorescent Art: Tucked away in the Jordaan neighbourhood, this museum is a surreal journey into the world of fluorescent and phosphorescent art. Be prepared to have your perception of colour and light challenged.

2. The Hash, Marijuana, and Hemp Museum: Amsterdam's cannabis culture is internationally known, and this museum, located on Oudezijds Achterburgwal, delves into the history and uses of cannabis throughout the ages.

Hidden Culinary Delights

In the city centre, you'll find a plethora of delightful dining experiences that often remain under the radar of mainstream tourism. These hidden culinary gems offer a taste of Amsterdam's local culture.

1. Café Papeneiland: Established in 1642, this charming café on the Prinsengracht canal is renowned for its delicious Dutch apple pie. Savour a slice in the cosy interior filled with antiques and old-world charm.

2. Café Chris: Located in the bustling Red Light District, Café Chris is an unassuming local haunt that serves up delicious Indonesian and Surinamese cuisine. It's a hidden spot for an affordable, flavourful meal.

Exploring Hidden Galleries

Amsterdam's art scene is not limited to its renowned museums; the city centre also hosts numerous hidden galleries, showcasing the works of local and international artists.

1. Eduard Planting Gallery: Situated on Eerste Bloemdwarsstraat, this photography gallery features a diverse range of contemporary and classic photography. It's an excellent place to discover new artistic perspectives.

2. Andenken Gallery: Nestled on Prinsengracht, this gallery specializes in urban and contemporary art, featuring a variety of works, from street art to pop surrelism. It's a unique and creative space.

The Charm of Canal-side Markets

While you're exploring the city centre, don't miss the opportunity to visit some of Amsterdam's charming canal-side markets. These vibrant markets offer a glimpse into local life and provide the perfect opportunity to pick up unique souvenirs.

1. Noordermarkt: Every Monday morning, the Noordermarkt comes to life with an organic farmers' market and an antique market. It's an excellent spot to find fresh produce and vintage treasures.

2. Lindengracht Market: Held every Saturday, this lively market on Lindengracht Street features a delightful array of stalls selling everything

from clothing to food. It's a great place to mingle with locals and soak up the atmosphere.

Summary

In the city centre of Amsterdam, hidden gems abound, waiting to be uncovered by intrepid urban explorers. From serene courtyards and historical house museums to quirky galleries and canal-side markets, the heart of the city is brimming with treasures that often go unnoticed. These are the gems that add depth and richness to your Amsterdam adventure, and they offer a unique opportunity to connect with the city's local culture and history. With this guide, you're well-prepared to embark on your exploration of Amsterdam's hidden treasures in the city centre.

Chapter 4: Amsterdam's Canal District

Prepare to be enchanted by the timeless allure of Amsterdam's iconic Canal District. In this chapter, we'll immerse ourselves in the grandeur and elegance of this UNESCO World Heritage site. With its historic canal houses, picturesque bridges, and charming waterways, this chapter provides a comprehensive guide to exploring the soul of Amsterdam's canal belt.

The Canal Belt: A UNESCO World Heritage Site

Stretching across the city like a graceful necklace, Amsterdam's canal belt is a defining feature of the city, earning its place as a UNESCO World Heritage site. The belt is a masterpiece of urban planning and architecture, conceived during the Dutch Golden Age of the 17th century. Comprising four main concentric canals, this area is a trove of historical and architectural treasures.

1. Herengracht (Gentlemen's Canal): The innermost canal, Herengracht, was once the exclusive domain of the city's most prosperous merchants. Today, its tree-lined banks are home to majestic canal houses and elegant townhouses.

2. Keizersgracht (Emperor's Canal): The Keizersgracht is the second of the main canals and is named after the Holy Roman Emperor Maximilian I. It boasts a blend of residential, commercial, and cultural spaces.

3. Prinsengracht (Prince's Canal): Prinsengracht, named after the Dutch prince, now King William II, showcases a diversity of architectural styles and contains some of the city's most famous landmarks.

4. Singelgracht (Singel Canal): The outermost canal, Singelgracht originally served as a moat around the city and was later incorporated into the canal belt. It is home to beautiful gardens and tranquil parks.

Exploring Canal Houses

One of the defining features of Amsterdam's canal district is its canal houses. These narrow, tall structures were designed with gabled facades and narrow frontages, a reflection of the city's history. As you explore, keep an eye out for unique architectural details:

1. Gable Stones: These ornate stones are often found above the entrances of canal houses and display various symbols and inscriptions that reveal the history and occupation of the original owner.

2. Hooks and Hoists: Many canal houses feature a pulley system, historically used to hoist goods and furniture to upper floors due to the narrow staircases.

3. Spouts and Downpipes: These decorative metal structures can be seen along the facades, used to divert rainwater from the roof into the canal. Each is a work of art in itself.

Canal Cruises: An Alternative Perspective

For a unique perspective of the canal district, consider taking a canal cruise. Various tour operators offer daytime and evening cruises that wind through the labyrinth of canals. These guided tours provide insights into the history, architecture, and culture of the area.

1. Daytime Cruises: Explore the canals under the warmth of the sun, where you can admire the canal houses, bridges, and landmarks from the water. Many tours also provide multilingual commentary to enhance your understanding of the city's history.

2. Evening Cruises: As the sun sets, the city's canals take on a magical aura. Evening cruises are particularly popular for romantic outings. You'll see the canal houses beautifully illuminated and pass under charmingly lit bridges.

Historic Canal-side Sites

The Canal District is home to several historic sites that offer a deeper understanding of Amsterdam's past.

1. Westerkerk: Located on Prinsengracht, Westerkerk is one of Amsterdam's most iconic churches. It dates back to the 17th century and offers visitors the chance to climb its tower for breath taking city views.

2. Anne Frank House: The Prinsengracht canal houses the Anne Frank House, where the young Jewish girl Anne Frank penned her world-famous diary during World War II. Visiting this site is a poignant and moving experience.

Hidden Gems along the Canals

Amsterdam's canal belt is not only about the grandeur of the main canals but also the charming side streets, bridges, and courtyards. As you stroll along the canals, take time to explore these hidden gems:

1. The Seven Bridges of Reguliersgracht: This enchanting spot is famous for its seven bridges in a row over Reguliersgracht, offering a picturesque photo opportunity.

2. The Begijnhof Courtyard: As mentioned in Chapter 3, the Begijnhof is a serene oasis hidden behind a nondescript entrance on Spui square, featuring stunning 17th-century houses and a quiet garden.

Dining by the Canals

To savour the ambiance of the canal belt, enjoy a meal at one of the many canal-side restaurants. These establishments offer both local and international cuisine, allowing you to dine with a view of the tranquil waterways.

1. Café de Jaren: Located on Nieuwe Doelenstraat, this modern café boasts a vast terrace overlooking the Amstel River. It's the perfect spot for a leisurely lunch or drinks with a view.

2. De Belhamel: Nestled on the Brouwersgracht, this fine-dining restaurant offers French-Mediterranean cuisine in a historic canal house. The elegant setting is a splendid choice for a special meal.

Summary

The Canal District is the jewel in Amsterdam's crown, and exploring it is an absolute must during your urban exploration adventure. With its UNESCO World Heritage status, canal houses steeped in history, and an abundance of hidden gems, this area offers a unique glimpse into the city's rich past and vibrant present. Whether you choose to wander along the canals, embark on a canal cruise, or dine with a view, the canal district is a living testament to Amsterdam's enduring charm. This chapter serves as your comprehensive guide, ensuring you make the most of your exploration of this exquisite neighbourhood.

Chapter 5: Local Culture and Traditions

Amsterdam's allure extends far beyond its picturesque canals and historic landmarks. It's a city with a rich tapestry of culture and traditions, blending old-world charm with a modern, cosmopolitan vibe. In this chapter, we'll delve deep into the essence of Amsterdam's local culture, its time-honoured traditions, and the vibrant celebrations that define the city's character. Uncover the beating heart of this unique metropolis.

Dutch Traditions and Festivals

Amsterdam is a city where traditions are cherished and celebrated. Understanding these local customs will enhance your urban exploration journey.

1. King's Day (Koningsdag): One of the most colourful and exuberant events in Amsterdam, King's Day is celebrated on April 27th, marking the birthday of King Willem-Alexander. The city turns into a sea of orange as locals and visitors don the national colour and participate in street markets, live music, and boat parades.

2. Sinterklaas: A beloved tradition, Sinterklaas (Saint Nicholas) arrives in Amsterdam in late November, with his helpers known as Zwarte Pieten (Black Petes). This holiday is celebrated with parades, gifts, and festivities for children and families.

3. Liberation Day (Bevrijdingsdag): On May 5th, Amsterdam joins the nation in commemorating the end of World War II. The city hosts concerts, exhibitions, and festivities to honour freedom and reflect on the country's history.

4. Tulip Season: Springtime in Amsterdam means the arrival of vibrant tulip blooms. Keukenhof Gardens, located just outside the city, is a spectacular destination to witness the vast array of tulips in full bloom.

The Influence of Art and Design

Amsterdam is a hub of creativity, and its influence in the world of art and design is profound. Here, you'll find a wealth of museums, galleries, and cultural landmarks that showcase this influence.

1. Rijksmuseum: The Rijksmuseum is a treasure trove of Dutch Golden Age art and history. It houses masterpieces by Rembrandt, Vermeer, and Van Gogh, among others. Exploring this museum is a deep dive into Dutch artistic heritage.

2. Stedelijk Museum: Modern and contemporary art enthusiasts will revel in the Stedelijk Museum's collection, which features works by artists like Mondrian, Kandinsky, and Picasso.

3. Dutch Design: The Netherlands has made significant contributions to design, and you can explore this heritage at various locations in Amsterdam. The Droog Design store and the Piet Hein Eek gallery are just two examples of spaces dedicated to contemporary Dutch design.

Music and Performance

Amsterdam's musical and performance scene is diverse, ranging from classical to contemporary. Immerse yourself in the city's harmonious culture.

1. Concertgebouw: Home to the Royal Concertgebouw Orchestra, this world-renowned concert hall offers an impressive line-up of classical music performances. The acoustics and ambiance of this venue are legendary.

2. Paradiso and Melkweg: For lovers of contemporary music, these two iconic venues host a variety of concerts, featuring both local and international artists across different genres.

Culinary Traditions

Dutch cuisine is hearty and flavourful, with dishes that showcase the country's maritime history. Delight your taste buds with traditional Dutch fare.

1. Dutch Pancakes: Dutch pancakes, known as pannenkoeken, are a delicious treat. They come in various forms, including sweet and savoury and are often enjoyed with toppings like syrup, cheese, or fruit.

2. Haring: Raw herring fish, served with onions and pickles, is a classic Dutch street food. Try it the local way by taking a bite instead of cutting it into pieces.

3. Dutch Cheese: The Netherlands is renowned for its cheese, and Gouda and Edam are just two examples of the country's cheese varieties. Explore local markets to sample and purchase these savoury delights.

Festivals and Cultural Hotspots

Amsterdam is a city of festivals and cultural events that provide a glimpse into the vibrant local scene. Here are some not to be missed:

1. Holland Festival: This international performing arts festival takes place in June and showcases a wide array of theatre, music, and dance performances, often with thought-provoking themes.

2. De Parade: A mobile theatre festival, De Parade travels through the Netherlands, setting up in various Dutch cities during the summer. It's a delightful blend of performing arts, food, and entertainment.

3. NDSM Werf: Located in the vibrant NDSM area, the NDSM Werf is a creative hotspot with cultural events, street art, and a bustling flea market.

Local Experiences

To immerse yourself in the local culture, consider participating in these authentic Amsterdam experiences:

1. Cheese Tasting: Visit local cheese shops to sample various Dutch cheeses and learn about their production.

2. Flower Market: Amsterdam's flower market is famous for its stunning tulip displays and provides a unique opportunity to purchase flower bulbs to take home.

3. Windmills: Take a short trip to the outskirts of Amsterdam to explore the historic windmills at Zaanse Schans and learn about traditional Dutch milling techniques.

Summary

Amsterdam's local culture and traditions are a vital part of the city's character, enriching your urban exploration journey with a profound understanding of the city's heritage and creativity. From centuries-old festivals to the influence of art and design, the city offers a diverse range of cultural experiences. This chapter serves as your guide to connecting with the local culture and traditions that make Amsterdam a truly unique destination. Whether you're savouring Dutch pancakes or witnessing world-class performances, you'll discover the authentic soul of this vibrant metropolis.

Chapter 6: The Unique Neighbourhoods

Amsterdam's charm lies not only in its iconic canals and historic centre but also in the diverse and unique neighbourhoods that make up this fascinating city. In this chapter, we'll take you on a journey through Amsterdam's distinctive districts, each with its own character, culture, and hidden treasures. Explore the local life, artistic enclaves, and picturesque corners of these extraordinary neighbourhoods.

De Pijp: A Bohemian Retreat

De Pijp is a vibrant neighbourhood, known for its bohemian atmosphere, eclectic mix of cultures, and lively streets. The district's heart, the Albert Cuyp Market, is a bustling street market offering an array of food stalls, fresh produce, and unique finds.

1. Albert Cuyp Market: This market, named after the 17th-century Dutch painter Albert Cuyp, is a sensory delight. Stroll through the stalls filled with everything from Dutch cheese to ethnic cuisine, fresh flowers, clothing, and handmade crafts. Don't forget to try the herring sandwich – a Dutch delicacy!

2. Sarphatipark: De Pijp is home to Sarphatipark, a serene green space named after Samuel Sarphati, a 19th-century physician and urban planner. It's perfect for a leisurely stroll or a picnic on a sunny day.

Jordaan: A Quaint Quarters of Canals

The Jordaan district is a charming and picturesque neighbourhood, famous for its narrow canals, historic houses, and quaint atmosphere. Once a working-class area, it's now a thriving cultural hub.

1. Anne Frank House: Situated on the Prinsengracht canal, the Anne Frank House is a museum dedicated to the Jewish girl Anne Frank, who documented her life in hiding during World War II. It's an incredibly moving and educational experience.

2. Noorderkerk: The Noorderkerk, or Northern Church, is an elegant Protestant church with a distinctive bell tower. The square around it is often used for markets, and it's a delightful spot for a leisurely stroll.

Oud-West: Hip and Happening

Oud-West is a district on the rise, known for its eclectic mix of cultures, creative scene, and vibrant ambiance. The area's streets are dotted with boutique shops, cosy cafes, and trendy eateries.

1. Foodhallen: This trendy food hall in an old tram depot features a variety of gourmet food stalls, making it a great place to sample diverse culinary delights.

2. De Hallen: A cultural hub in Oud-West, De Hallen is a former tram depot transformed into a centre for art, culture, and entertainment. You'll find boutique shops, a cinema, and art exhibitions here.

De Plantage: Green and Cultural Haven

De Plantage is a green oasis within Amsterdam, home to cultural gems, historical landmarks, and lush gardens. It's a peaceful retreat in the midst of the city's hustle and bustle.

1. Artis Royal Zoo: Artis is one of the oldest zoos in Europe, founded in 1838. In addition to a wide variety of animals, it houses a beautiful botanical garden, a planetarium, and a museum.

2. Hortus Botanicus: This botanical garden is one of the oldest in the world and is a tranquil place to wander amid an impressive collection of plants from around the globe.

De Baarsjes: Up-and-Coming

De Baarsjes is a lively and up-and-coming neighbourhood known for it multicultural atmosphere, colourful street art, and a sense of community It's a neighbourhood that has undergone a recent transformation, with numerous hotspots emerging.

1. Food Truck Festival: During the summer, De Baarsjes hosts a lively food truck festival where you can sample a wide variety of international cuisines and enjoy live music.

2. Street Art: De Baarsjes boasts a vibrant street art scene, with striking murals and graffiti adorning its buildings. Take a walking tour to explore these colourful expressions.

Amsterdam Noord: Creative and Contemporary

Across the IJ River lies Amsterdam Noord, a district that's undergone a significant transformation in recent years. It's a hub for contemporary art, cultural events, and innovative architecture.

1. EYE Filmmuseum: This iconic film museum on the banks of the river is an architectural marvel. It offers an extensive collection of films and hosts film-related events, exhibitions, and screenings.

2. A'DAM Lookout: Visit the A'DAM Lookout tower for breath taking panoramic views of the city. It also features Europe's highest swing, a daring experience for the adventurous.

Summary

Amsterdam's unique neighbourhoods are a testament to the city's diversity and dynamism. De Pijp's bohemian charm, Jordaan's picturesque canals, Oud-West's hip and happening scene, De Plantage's cultural richness, De Baarsjes' up-and-coming spirit, and Amsterdam Noord's creative energy all offer a distinctive perspective on the city. Exploring these neighbourhoods is a delightful journey through Amsterdam's local life, artistic expressions, and hidden treasures. With this chapter as your guide, you're ready to immerse yourself in the diverse tapestry of this remarkable city. Each neighbourhood tells a different story, waiting for you to discover its unique charm and cultural riches.

Chapter 7: Amsterdam's Hidden Waterways

Amsterdam's appeal goes far beyond its well-known canals. In this chapter, we'll delve into the city's hidden waterways, exploring its lesser-known canals, tranquil lakes, and enchanting rivers. Embark on a journey through the quieter, more secluded aquatic realms of Amsterdam, revealing the hidden treasures that are often overlooked.

Amstel River: The Lifeblood of Amsterdam

The Amstel River is the beating heart of Amsterdam, yet it often remains overshadowed by its more famous canal counterparts. As you follow its course, you'll discover a sense of serenity and a different perspective on the city.

1. Amstelpark: This spacious park is situated on the banks of the Amstel River, offering a serene escape from the urban bustle. You can enjoy scenic walks, picnics, and a variety of horticultural gardens.

2. Magere Brug (Skinny Bridge): This iconic bridge gracefully stretches across the Amstel River and is beautifully illuminated at night. It's a perfect spot for a romantic evening stroll.

The Nieuwe Meer: A Hidden Gem

The Nieuwe Meer is a tranquil lake located to the southwest of Amsterdam. It's a lesser-known aquatic paradise that provides a peaceful retreat from the city's hustle and bustle.

1. Beaches: Along the shores of Nieuwe Meer, you'll find artificial beaches where locals gather to sunbathe and swim during the summer months. It's a hidden oasis for relaxation and recreation.

2. Water sports: The Nieuwe Meer is a haven for water sports enthusiasts. You can indulge in activities like windsurfing, paddle boarding, and sailing in this scenic and serene environment.

Zeeburg: A Hidden Waterfront

Zeeburg is a fascinating area located to the east of Amsterdam, where you can uncover the city's maritime history and enjoy the soothing atmosphere of the IJmeer.

1. IJburg: IJburg is a modern neighbourhood built on artificial islands in the IJmeer. It offers a beautiful stretch of beach, a bustling harbour, and a variety of waterside dining options.

2. Blijburg: Blijburg aan Zee is a popular city beach located on IJburg. It's a vibrant place with a sandy shore, lively events, and beachfront restaurants.

The Western Islands: A Peaceful Escape

The Western Islands, or Westelijke Eilanden, are a cluster of islands in the Western Harbor area of Amsterdam. This hidden gem is a tranquil escape from the urban commotion.

1. Prinseneiland: Prinseneiland is one of the islands, known for its charming canals, historic warehouses, and serene ambiance. Take a leisurely stroll to appreciate its unique atmosphere.

2. Westerdok: Westerdok is another of the Western Islands, and its home to a marina and picturesque views. It's a peaceful place for a waterside walk.

Amsterdamse Bos: A Natural Haven

Amsterdamse Bos, or Amsterdam Forest, is a vast green oasis on the outskirts of the city. It's a hidden treasure that provides an escape into nature without leaving Amsterdam.

1. Lakes and Ponds: The Amsterdamse Bos features several lakes and ponds where you can enjoy rowing, swimming, and picnicking. The Grote Vijver is a particularly popular spot.

2. Forest Walks: The forest offers numerous walking trails, and you can explore its diverse flora and fauna. Keep an eye out for deer, Highland cattle, and Shetland ponies.

Noorderpark: An Urban Sanctuary

Noorderpark is an urban park located in Amsterdam North, providing a serene retreat in the heart of the city.

1. Noorderparkbad: In the summer, the Noorderparkbad outdoor swimming pool is a favourite spot for locals to cool off and soak up the sun. It's an ideal place for a refreshing swim.

2. Noorderparkkamer: This community-driven venue hosts cultural events and art exhibitions. It's a unique space where locals gather for a sense of community and creativity.

Oostelijk Havengebied: Architectural Marvels

The Oostelijk Havengebied, or Eastern Docklands, is a modern and architecturally striking district in the eastern part of Amsterdam. It's a hidden gem for those interested in contemporary design and innovation.

1. Java Island: Java Island is an architectural marvel with a distinct urban design. Its innovative buildings and waterfront promenades provide a glimpse into Amsterdam's future.

2. Cruquius Island: Once an industrial area, Cruquius Island is being transformed into a sustainable and lively neighbourhood with a focus on urban agriculture and community initiatives.

Summary

While Amsterdam's famous canals are undoubtedly a highlight of the city, its hidden waterways offer a different kind of charm and tranquillity. Whether it's the serene Amstel River, the tranquil Nieuwe Meer, or the modern marvels of the Eastern Docklands, these hidden aquatic gems provide a unique perspective on Amsterdam. With this chapter as your guide, you're ready to embark on a journey through the quieter, lesser-known waters of the city,

Uncovering its hidden treasures and experiencing a sense of peace and wonder that often escapes the bustling urban explorer.

Chapter 8: Amsterdam's Artistic Heritage

Amsterdam's vibrant artistic heritage is deeply woven into the fabric of the city, making it a cultural mecca for art lovers from around the world. In this chapter, we'll guide you through the rich tapestry of Amsterdam's art scene, exploring its world-class museums, influential artists, and the dynamic contemporary art movement. Embark on a journey through the city's artistic legacy, unveiling its hidden treasures and creative wonders.

Rijksmuseum: The Crown Jewel of Dutch Art

The Rijksmuseum stands as a beacon of Dutch art and history, housing an unparalleled collection of masterpieces that span centuries. It's not only a museum but a journey through the rich tapestry of the Netherlands.

1. The Night Watch: Rembrandt's monumental painting "The Night Watch" is a masterpiece that commands the attention of every visitor. It's a vivid representation of Dutch Golden Age art.

2. The Milkmaid: Johannes Vermeer's "The Milkmaid" is a testament to his skill in capturing everyday life with a mesmerizing subtlety that's quintessentially Dutch.

3. The Dolls' House: A hidden treasure, this 17th-century dolls' house is a stunning miniature representation of Dutch domestic life, filled with intricate details and secrets to discover.

Van Gogh Museum: A Glimpse into the Artist's Soul

The Van Gogh Museum is a testament to the tormented genius of Vincent van Gogh. It's a journey through his life, from his early works to his post-Impressionist masterpieces.

1. Sunflowers: "Sunflowers" is one of Van Gogh's most iconic works, renowned for its vivid colours and powerful expression. It's a must-see painting that encapsulates his artistry.

2. The Bedroom: Van Gogh's "The Bedroom" series showcases his ability to transform ordinary scenes into powerful expressions of emotion and colour.

3. Van Gogh's Letters: The museum also houses an extensive collection of the artist's letters, providing a deep insight into his life, thoughts, and creative process.

Stedelijk Museum: Modern and Contemporary Marvels

The Stedelijk Museum is Amsterdam's contemporary art hub, featuring an impressive collection of modern and contemporary art, design, and applied arts.

1. De Stijl Movement: The museum showcases the works of the De Stijl movement, founded by Piet Mondrian. The movement's philosophy of simplicity and abstraction is evident in its art.

2. Contemporary Installations: The Stedelijk frequently hosts contemporary art installations, providing a glimpse into the cutting-edge of the art world.

Moco Museum: Street Art and Contemporary Icons

The Moco Museum is a celebration of contemporary art and culture, featuring works by iconic artists and provocative street art.

1. Banksy: The museum houses an extensive collection of Banksy's thought-provoking and politically charged art.

2. Pop Art: Works by renowned pop artists like Andy Warhol, Roy Lichtenstein, and Keith Haring are on display, highlighting the global influence of pop culture.

Rembrandt House Museum: The Master's Studio

The Rembrandt House Museum is the former home of the iconic Dutch painter Rembrandt van Rijn. It provides a unique opportunity to step into his world.

1. Studio Reconstruction: The museum features a reconstructed studio, offering a glimpse into Rembrandt's creative process and tools.

2. Etchings: You'll find an extensive collection of Rembrandt's etchings, showcasing his remarkable skill in printmaking.

Cobra Museum: Avant-Garde and Experimental Art

The Cobra Museum celebrates the Cobra movement, a post-World War II avant-garde art movement that embraced spontaneity and experimentation.

1. Asger Jorn: Explore works by Asger Jorn, one of the founders of the Cobra movement, known for his abstract and vibrant art.

2. Constant Nieuwenhuys: The museum also houses works by Constant Nieuwenhuys, who played a crucial role in the development of the Cobra movement.

Hidden Galleries and Street Art

Amsterdam's art scene extends beyond its famous museums. The city's streets and hidden galleries are home to a thriving street art and contemporary art culture.

1. Street Art Walking Tours: Embark on a street art walking tour in neighbourhoods like Noord and the Jordaan to explore vibrant street art.

2. Art Galleries in Jordaan: Jordaan is home to numerous art galleries showcasing contemporary and traditional art. Stroll along its streets to discover hidden gems.

Summary

Amsterdam's artistic heritage is a tapestry of masterpieces, movements, and creative expressions that define the city's cultural identity. From the grandeur of the Rijksmuseum and the intimate insights into Van Gogh's life to the contemporary provocations of the Moco Museum, this chapter has been your guide to the city's artistic wonders. Whether you're exploring classic art or contemporary creations, Amsterdam's artistic treasures await your discovery, ready to inspire and enrich your urban exploration journey.

Chapter 9: Amsterdam's Cultural Festivals

Amsterdam's cultural calendar is brimming with vibrant festivals that celebrate the city's diversity and creativity. In this chapter, we will lead you through a year-round journey of music, arts, and traditions. Uncover the unique and exhilarating festivals that colour the streets and canals of Amsterdam.

Amsterdam Dance Event (ADE): The Electronic Extravaganza

Amsterdam Dance Event is the world's leading electronic music conference and festival. Every October, the city transforms into a dance music mecca, attracting DJs, producers, and music enthusiasts from around the globe.

1. Daytime Program: ADE features a comprehensive daytime program of conferences, workshops, and talks, exploring the current state and future of electronic music.

2. Night-time Festival: As the sun sets, ADE turns into a massive festival, with events happening in over 200 venues across Amsterdam. Prepare to dance to the hottest electronic beats.

Tulip Festival: Blooms across the City

In spring, Amsterdam bursts into colour with the Tulip Festival. Over 500,000 tulips in various locations throughout the city create a stunning display of floral artistry.

1. Locations: Discover tulip displays in iconic locations like the Rijksmuseum, Keukenhof Gardens, and various neighbourhoods, including the Jordaan and De Pijp.

2. Thematic Displays: The Tulip Festival often follows a specific theme each year, adding an artistic and creative touch to the city's gardens.

Kingsland Festival: Koningsdag Extravaganza

Kingsland Festival is a vibrant celebration of King's Day (Koningsdag), held on April 27th. It's one of the largest and most energetic outdoor festivals in the city.

1. Musical Line-up: Kingsland hosts a stellar line-up of international and local DJs, making it a must-visit for electronic music enthusiasts.

2. Multiple Locations: The festival takes place simultaneously in multiple Dutch cities, with Amsterdam's edition being a standout event.

Amsterdam Light Festival: Illuminating the Canals

The Amsterdam Light Festival takes place during the winter months, turning the city's canals into an enchanting open-air light exhibition.

1. Light Installations: Artists from around the world create captivating light installations, illuminating the canals and the city's historic sites.

2. Canal Cruises: One of the best ways to experience the festival is by taking a canal cruise that guides you through the stunning displays.

Uitmarkt: Cultural Kick-off

The Uitmarkt marks the start of the cultural season in the Netherlands. This free event offers a glimpse of the country's cultural offerings, from music and dance to theatre and literature.

1. Stages and Performances: Multiple stages are set up around the city, hosting a variety of performances and showcasing the nation's talent.

2. Information Stands: Get insights into the upcoming cultural season and connect with artists and cultural institutions at information stands.

Grachtenfestival: Classical Music on the Canals

The Grachtenfestival, or Canal Festival, is a classical music festival that takes place in August. It combines the beauty of Amsterdam's canals with the elegance of classical music.

1. Canal Concerts: Classical concerts are held on stages floating on the city's waterways, creating a unique and unforgettable musical experience.

2. Young Talent: The festival also highlights the talents of young musicians, adding an element of innovation to the classical music scene.

Kwaku Festival: A Taste of Suriname

The Kwaku Festival is a celebration of Surinamese culture and cuisine. It's a lively event featuring food stalls, music, and dance.

1. Culinary Delights: Sample a wide variety of Surinamese dishes, from roti to bara, and experience the diverse flavours of this South American cuisine.

2. Music and Dance: Kwaku Festival boasts a vibrant line-up of live music, including genres like kaseko, kawina, and zouk.

Pluk de Nacht: Open-Air Cinema

Pluk de Nacht is a free open-air film festival held during the summer months. It showcases a selection of international independent films, documentaries, and shorts.

1. Unique Locations: Films are screened in unconventional locations such as an old industrial shipyard or a beach setting, creating an immersive movie experience.

2. Special Screenings: Pluk de Nacht often includes premieres and Q&A sessions with filmmakers, adding an interactive element to the festival.

Summary

Amsterdam's cultural festivals offer a kaleidoscope of experiences celebrating music, arts, traditions, and creativity year-round. Whether you're dancing to electronic beats at ADE, basking in the tulip display of the Tulip Festival, or exploring the city's canals illuminated by the Amsterdam Light Festival, this chapter has been your guide to the city's most exhilarating and culturally rich festivals. From classical music on the canals to open-air cinema by the beach, Amsterdam's festival scene invites you to immerse yourself in the heart of its vibrant cultural tapestry.

Chapter 10: Amsterdam's Culinary Odyssey

Amsterdam's culinary scene is a delightful journey through diverse flavours, international influences, and innovative dining experiences. In this chapter, we will lead you on a gastronomic adventure through the city's restaurants, street food markets, and local delicacies. Savour the delectable offerings and discover the culinary gems that make Amsterdam a food lover's paradise.

Dutch Delights: A Taste of Tradition

Dutch cuisine is a hearty reflection of the country's history and maritime heritage. Dive into the traditional Dutch dishes that offer a taste of the Netherlands.

1. Dutch Pancakes: Dutch pancakes, or pannenkoeken, come in various forms, from sweet with toppings like syrup, cheese, and fruit to savoury with ingredients like bacon and cheese. Try them at local pancake houses.

2. Haring: Raw herring fish, served with onions and pickles, is a classic Dutch street food. For an authentic experience, take a bite instead of cutting it into pieces.

3. Bitterballen: These crispy, deep-fried meat-based snacks are a Dutch favourite, often served with mustard for dipping. Enjoy them in a cosy Dutch pub, known as a bruin café.

Surinamese and Indonesian Influences

Amsterdam's culinary scene is enriched by the Surinamese and Indonesian influences, thanks to its colonial history. Explore the flavours of these vibrant cuisines.

1. Rijsttafel: An Indonesian rijsttafel is a culinary journey featuring a variety of dishes, from spicy satay to fragrant rendang. Many Indonesian restaurants in Amsterdam offer this delightful feast.

2. Roti: Surinamese roti, a soft flatbread served with curried vegetables and meats, is a flavourful and satisfying dish. Visit local Surinamese eateries to enjoy this unique creation.

Cheese, Please!

The Netherlands is renowned for its cheese, and Amsterdam is the perfect place to sample and purchase these savoury delights.

1. Cheese Markets: While traditional cheese markets can be found in towns like Alkmaar, you can also visit the cheese shops and markets in Amsterdam to sample and purchase varieties like Gouda and Edam.

2. Cheese Tasting: Many local cheese shops offer tastings, allowing you to explore the nuances of Dutch cheese and find your favourites.

Global Flavours in Amsterdam

Amsterdam's cosmopolitan character is reflected in its diverse range of international cuisine. Discover a world of flavours within the city's streets.

1. Leidseplein and Leidsestraat: These areas are known for their international dining options, from Mediterranean and Asian to Middle Eastern and South American.

2. Food Halls: Food halls like Foodhallen and De Hallen offer a variety of international cuisines under one roof. It's a great way to sample diverse flavours in a single visit.

Amsterdam's Markets: A Culinary Feast

Amsterdam's markets are a culinary treasure trove, offering a wide range of fresh produce, street food, and local delicacies.

1. Albert Cuyp Market: This bustling street market in De Pijp offers everything from Dutch cheese and fresh herring to exotic spices and clothing.

2. Noordermarkt: The Noordermarkt features an organic farmers' market on Saturdays and an antiques and curiosities market on Mondays. It's an ideal spot to discover local produce and artisanal goods.

3. Dappermarkt: Located in the diverse Oost district, Dappermarkt is a multicultural market offering a diverse array of foods, clothing, and more.

Amsterdam's Sweet Treats

Indulge your sweet tooth with a range of Dutch and international confections that will satisfy your cravings.

1. Stroopwafels: Stroopwafels are thin, syrup-filled waffle cookies that are a beloved Dutch snack. You can find them at local markets and specialty shops.

2. Dutch Liquorice: The Netherlands is known for its liquorice, with a wide range of flavours and textures. Try both sweet and salty varieties to discover your preference.

3. Chocolate Boutiques: Explore Amsterdam's artisanal chocolate boutiques, like Puccini Bomboni and Metropolitan, to savour handmade chocolates and truffles.

Michelin-Starred Excellence

Amsterdam boasts several Michelin-starred restaurants, each offering a culinary experience to remember.

1. De Librije: De Librije, a three-Michelin-star restaurant, offers a gourmet journey with a focus on seasonal, regional ingredients.

2. Ciel Bleu: Located on the 23rd floor of Hotel Okura, Ciel Bleu is known for its inventive cuisine, stunning views, and two Michelin stars.

Craft Beer and Jenever: A Toast to Tradition

Amsterdam's craft beer and jenever (Dutch gin) scene is flourishing. Sample traditional and innovative drinks at local breweries and distilleries.

1. Brouwerij 't IJ: This windmill brewery in the city is famous for its craft beers, and you can enjoy a tasting in the cosy pub next door.

2. Jenever Bars: Explore jenever bars in Amsterdam like Wynand Fockink, where you can savour this classic Dutch spirit.

Summary

Amsterdam's culinary scene is a flavourful tapestry that weaves together traditional Dutch dishes, global influences, and innovative dining experiences. Whether you're savouring Dutch pancakes, indulging in Surinamese roti, or exploring the international flavours of the city, Amsterdam's gastronomy offers a delectable journey for food enthusiasts. From street markets to Michelin-starred restaurants, the city's culinary delights are ready to satisfy your palate and add a savoury dimension to your urban exploration journey.

Chapter 11: Amsterdam by Night

As the sun dips below the horizon, Amsterdam undergoes a mesmerizing transformation, casting a nocturnal spell over its enchanting streets and canals. In this chapter, we'll guide you through the city's vibrant nightlife, from its lively bars and clubs to its elegant evening experiences. Embark on an exploration of Amsterdam after dark, where the city comes alive with a unique and dynamic energy.

Amsterdam's Nightlife: A Tale of Two Cities

Amsterdam's nightlife offers a spectrum of experiences, from laid-back bars and cosy pubs to energetic clubs and elegant cocktail lounges. Let's explore the city's diverse nocturnal landscape.

1. Brown Cafés: Start your evening in one of Amsterdam's traditional brown cafés, characterized by their warm and cosy atmosphere. These old-world pubs are perfect for a leisurely drink and conversation.

2. Cocktail Bars: If you prefer a touch of elegance, Amsterdam's cocktail bars, such as Door 74 and Tales & Spirits, offer expertly crafted drinks in a sophisticated setting.

3. Nightclubs: The city's nightclubs, like De School and Shelter, come to life in the late hours with a blend of electronic music, live performances, and dancing that continues into the early morning.

Red Light District: An Iconic Experience

Amsterdam's Red Light District is known for its distinctive character, vibrant nightlife, and a bit of the city's provocative charm.

1. Window Shopping: Stroll through the narrow alleys and canals, where you'll encounter the infamous windows lit with red neon. It's an experience unique to Amsterdam's night scene.

2. Night Tours: Explore the area with guided night tours that provide a historical perspective and a deeper understanding of this iconic neighbourhood.

Live Music and Concerts

Amsterdam is a city of music lovers, and its stages host an array of live performances, from intimate jazz clubs to grand concert halls.

1. Paradiso: This former church turned concert venue is a legendary spot for live music, hosting a variety of genres, from rock and pop to electronic and world music.

2. Bimhuis: Jazz enthusiasts should head to Bimhuis, a renowned venue that showcases jazz artists from around the world in an intimate setting with excellent acoustics.

Amsterdam's Canal Cruises: Illuminated Adventures

Amsterdam's canal cruises aren't limited to the daytime. After dark, these journeys offer a magical perspective of the city, as its historic sites and iconic bridges are illuminated.

1. Candlelit Cruises: Several companies offer candlelit evening cruises with dinner and drinks, providing an enchanting experience on the water.

2. Amsterdam Light Festival Cruises: If you're visiting during the winter months, Amsterdam's Light Festival offers canal cruises that guide you through the illuminated artworks along the waterways.

Late-Night Eateries and Snacks

After a night of exploration, satisfy your hunger with a range of late-night eateries, offering everything from Dutch snacks to international delights.

1. Febo: A quintessential Dutch experience, Febo is a chain of fast-food restaurants with coin-operated vending machines where you can purchase croquettes and other snacks.

2. Late-Night Frites: Friteries across the city stay open late, serving fresh-cut fries with a variety of sauces, including the classic Dutch fritesaus.

Amsterdam's Jazz and Blues Bars

For a soulful and relaxed evening, Amsterdam's jazz and blues bars provide the perfect setting for live performances and smooth sounds.

1. Maloe Melo: This cosy brown café is a popular spot for blues lovers, featuring live music and a relaxed atmosphere.

2. Bourbon Street: Bourbon Street is an iconic jazz and blues bar in the heart of Amsterdam, hosting both international and local acts.

Late-Night Shopping and Markets

Amsterdam's shopping scene doesn't sleep. Discover late-night markets and stores that cater to night owls.

1. Albert Heijn: Some Albert Heijn supermarkets in Amsterdam are open until midnight, allowing you to pick up groceries or snacks for your evening.

2. Night Markets: Explore night markets like the Dappermarkt, which offers extended shopping hours on certain days.

Summary

Amsterdam by night is a dynamic and enchanting world, where the city's diverse nightlife comes alive. Whether you're sipping cocktails in elegant lounges, dancing the night away in lively nightclubs, or exploring the iconic Red Light District, Amsterdam offers an array of nocturnal experiences. You can also unwind on candlelit canal cruises, soak in live music performances, and satisfy your late-night cravings with delicious snacks. As the city's lights come on and the streets take on a new energy, Amsterdam invites you to be a part of its captivating nightlife, where each night holds a story waiting to be told.

Chapter 12: Amsterdam's Green Escapes

Amsterdam's enchanting green spaces offer a serene escape from the city's urban hustle and bustle. In this chapter, we'll guide you through the lush parks, tranquil gardens, and natural havens that grace the city. Embark on a journey through Amsterdam's green escapes, discovering the hidden oases that provide a breath of fresh air and a sense of tranquillity.

Vondelpark: Amsterdam's Crown Jewel of Greenery

Vondelpark is the city's most famous and beloved park, a lush and expansive green oasis in the heart of Amsterdam.

1. Stroll and Picnic: Take a leisurely walk along winding paths, relax on the grass, and enjoy a picnic in this vibrant park, offering a sense of tranquillity amidst the urban bustle.

2. Open-Air Theatre: In the summer months, the Vondelpark Openluchttheater hosts a variety of cultural events, from music performances to theatre shows, creating a lively atmosphere.

Keukenhof Gardens: A Floral Extravaganza

Keukenhof, located just a short drive from Amsterdam, is one of the world's most renowned flower gardens, showcasing millions of tulips, daffodils, and other spring blooms.

1. Tulip Season: Visit Keukenhof during the spring (usually March to May) to witness the mesmerizing sea of colourful flowers that blankets the landscape.

2. Themed Gardens: Explore themed gardens, such as the Historical Garden and Natural Garden, offering a variety of horticultural wonders.

Westerpark: A Green Gem in the West

Westerpark is a vibrant and trendy park located in the western part of Amsterdam, known for its green expanses, cultural venues, and relaxing atmosphere.

1. Sunday Market: On the first Sunday of each month, the Westerpark hosts a lively market with stalls offering food, fashion, and unique crafts.

2. The Machinegebouw: This industrial-style building houses a restaurant and event spaces, creating a perfect blend of history and modernity.

Hortus Botanicus: Amsterdam's Botanical Gem

Hortus Botanicus is a historic botanical garden in the heart of the city, offering a peaceful escape and a fascinating collection of rare plants.

1. Plant Diversity: Explore an array of exotic and indigenous plants, including tropical and subtropical species, cacti, and succulents.

2. Butterfly Greenhouse: The butterfly greenhouse in Hortus Botanicus allows you to observe these delicate creatures up close, making it a captivating experience for visitors of all ages.

Beatrixpark: A Hidden Oasis

Beatrixpark is a lesser-known, tranquil park in the southern part of Amsterdam, providing a peaceful retreat away from the city's crowds.

1. Serene Lake: A beautiful lake graces the park, offering an ideal spot for a leisurely stroll or a peaceful picnic by the water's edge.

2. Sculptures and Art: The Park features various sculptures and art installations that add an artistic touch to the natural landscape.

Amsterdamse Bos: The City's Forest

Amsterdamse Bos, or Amsterdam Forest, is a vast and diverse forested area on the outskirts of the city, offering a range of outdoor activities and natural beauty.

1. Boating and Swimming: Enjoy rowing on one of the forest's many lakes or take a dip in the Grote Vijver, a popular spot for swimming.

2. Forest Walks: Amsterdamse Bos boasts numerous walking trails, allowing you to explore the forest's rich flora and fauna, including Highland cattle and Shetland ponies.

Oosterpark: A Melting Pot of Cultures

Oosterpark, situated in the eastern part of Amsterdam, is known for its diverse atmosphere, with events and gatherings that reflect the city's multicultural character.

1. Festivals and Events: Oosterpark hosts various cultural events and festivals, making it a lively hub of activity throughout the year.

2. The National Slavery Monument: This important monument in the park serves as a memorial to the victims of slavery, providing a reflective space within the green surroundings.

Sloterplas: Waterfront Serenity

Sloterplas is a large lake in Amsterdam's western suburbs, offering a peaceful waterfront escape with recreational opportunities.

1. Beaches: Relax on the sandy shores of Sloterplas during the summer, and take a dip in the lake to cool off on a warm day.

2. Water sports: The Lake is ideal for water sports like windsurfing and sailing, allowing you to enjoy the refreshing breeze off the water.

Gaasperplas: A Nature Haven

Gaasperplas is a serene lake and nature park in the south-eastern part of Amsterdam, providing an idyllic environment for relaxation and outdoor activities.

1. Bird watching: The Park is a haven for birdwatchers, with various species of waterfowl and migratory birds that can be observed throughout the year.

2. Gaasperplas Festival: The annual Gaasperplas Festival offers music, culture, and food in the midst of this natural wonderland, creating a unique and harmonious blend of art and nature.

Summary

Amsterdam's green escapes offer a tranquil respite from the city's urban pace, from the iconic beauty of Vondelpark to the serene nature of Gaasperplas. Whether you're strolling through lush gardens, exploring cultural venues, or simply unwinding in a peaceful park, Amsterdam's green spaces provide a breath of fresh air and a sense of serenity. This chapter has been your guide to discovering these hidden oases within the city, inviting you to embrace the natural beauty and tranquillity that complements your urban exploration journey.

Don't miss out!

Visit the website below and you can sign up to receive emails whenever PA BOOKS publishes a new book. There's no charge and no obligation.

https://books2read.com/r/B-A-STTAB-MVZPC

BOOKS 2 READ

Connecting independent readers to independent writers.

Also by PA BOOKS

Hogan's Key

Kimberly & the Five Strange Goldfishes

The Enchanted Library

The Misadventures of Pirate Pete

From Wheel To Web: 40 Remarkable Inventions

Once Upon A Sleepy Time

The Global Game - The Evolution Of Football

Strides To Success: A Beginner's Guide to Running

The ChatGPT Handbook

Climate Crossroads

1000 Everyday Life Hacks

Urban Exploration - London The Comprehensive Travel Guide

Urban Exploration - New York The Comprehensive Travel Guide

Urban Exploration - Amsterdam The Comprehensive Travel Guide

Urban Exploration - Dubai The Comprehensive Travel Guide

Urban Exploration - Paris The Comprehensive Travel Guide

Milton Keynes UK
Ingram Content Group UK Ltd.
UKHW041820211123
432980UK00001BB/88

9 798223 085515